BLEED

BLEED

VIPUL RIKHI

Hawakal Publishers

Published by Hawakal Publishers, 185, Kali Temple Road, Nimta,
Calcutta 700049 India

Website: www.hawakal.com
Contact: info@hawakal.com

First edition (Paperback): September 2018

Printed and bound at S. P. Communications, Calcutta

Cover concept & design: Bitan Chakraborty

ISBN-13: 978-93-87883-33-8

Price: INR 350.00 | USD 10.99

for Shabnam

FOREWORD

Maps are of different kinds but they are usually made to highlight the significant details of a landscape. *Bleed* has the quality of a map yet it guides readers through an unchartered territory of a way to nowhere in particular. In the poem "The Traveller" Vipul writes that he is

> a traveller in nowhere and no place
> doing nothing
> at no time, with no body

He is "seeking nothing" but undeniably he is moving as "a traveller on his way..."

It is not a map that makes the pathway more straight forward but gives the reader a glimpse of what such a journey might demand — humour, emptiness, endlessly beginning afresh, lightness, a delight in surprise and above all savage honesty. The diversions and distractions from the path lie in 'busy-ness' and engaging with the party of make-up and make-believe of facades that shelve maturity.

In many of the poems there is a sense of Vipul's own struggle to acknowledge and excavate the words that describe the hidden layers of loneliness which are so close and yet distant from a sense of oneness.

Many of the poems take the form of a dialogue: a conversation with fragments of the self, with otherness and the elusive "heart of fire." In "The Garden" there is a playful but deeply-felt invitation to the lover, the companion to "walk into the garden of my attention..." This gives a sense that the self becomes alive in and through relationship and not in isolation. Some of the most evocative poems touch on the transcendence of the shared, ordinary moment.

Two chairs in a garden and two cups of tea
this is my idea of bliss
two-cup-full of slurp and then a kiss...
("Bliss 2")

There is sharpness in a number of the images that cut through a hazy, lazy claim to an easy resolution such as in "Secret Places." Sometimes this becomes a disarming self-mockery as in the recipe for unveiling an uncomfortable awareness in "Undoing."

Here Vipul urges himself and the reader to "take a piece of your heart and pound/ it thoroughly with your head that's shaken," but the search is in earnest and not frayed by cynicism.

Following the Google map to a named destination through a digitalized voice giving impersonal directions so that you no longer have a sense of place, direction or connection is a very different experience from these poems that take us on a journey.

Vipul's voice speaks directly to readers about a shared quest in response to an uncertain but unavoidable calling. W.H. Auden describes poetry as "paying homage by naming," and some of the landmarks have been powerfully named. "Bleed" sings of "the river of red/ That pumps into all human hearts/ an ocean that connects us all..."

Jane Sahi
May 2017

[Jane is a poet, writer and educationist. Deeply inspired by Gandhiji's educational vision and values, she founded the Sita School in the outskirts of Bangalore in 1975.]

CONTENTS

Poems
Revised Memories
[2002-2017]

BLEED

Bleeding is a must
Whether at first thrust
Or the monthly installment to repay
On the debt of life

One must bleed from cuts, gashes and the violence
Of the unjust
The heart in silence
But the wound must turn the colour of rust

Everyone bleeds
Everyone weeps blood
Everyone trusts

And all the bleeding one can do
All the blood that must burst
From veins and pipes and eyes
And mouth

Turns into a river of red
That pumps into all human hearts
An ocean that connects us all

And who can say they alone
Are just?
Who by themselves can claim a lust
For life?

This blood is primordial
Mother and wife
Gaia, Eve, Shakti, Earth

Do you imagine it's just
A liquid commodity
Sold by type?

Bleed, for it's an act
Of the spirit
That keeps us alive

WHERE WAS I LOOKING?

Where was I looking when love flew out of the window?
I was looking at the house, its walls,
the dead cement.
It must have perched for a moment
on the window-sill, looking
naively inside
with its innocent eyes—
but I hardly had time

My house of dreams is as big as the house I stay in
but not nearly so dreary
in fact it is splendid
and then it is time to end it
The Dream.

The bird is finally free in the sky
soaring
it is the eagle that is pouring
great black wings on the great blue sky
floating
on air as if it were water
its arms my arms
that could have been
(would like to be)

My arms busy sweeping
the window-sill, and shutting
the glass frames.

ALL DAY…

All day I have kept your memory near at hand
The clear bright vision of a yet untouched land

It shatters at the touch, liquid and shy
Full of fretful caresses the day goes by

I stoop to pluck the roses of my memory of your eyes
(within hand they lie)

The downpour of your absence waves like a hand
Appearing and disappearing like crabs in the sand

A LITTLE MORE SPACE

I need a little more space in my heart
Could we move things around a little?
The crucial things are the china parts
Where do I keep them, they're so brittle?

I certainly don't need more room for desires
They take up too much space already
I need more wood to light other fires
I need a whole forest to keep them steady

I need a little corner for a bird with its beak
Should I move the dressing-table of my wife?
I need a small mountain with a vertiginous peak
Can I shift the basic coordinates of my life?

YOU!

You run through my blood, seep down to my depths
Sucking my soul right out of its bolts
You till my distress
You line my soles

All the grime gathered up inside them
Speaks of you in unspeakable chime
You blow up my heart
Detonate my mind

To speak of you is to undescribe you
You sweat from my pores, and fall with my hair
No me to look, no you to find
This device is beyond repair

DREAM

I dreamed a dream of stone
Carved into a sunlit bone
Bright in colour, deep in tone

I dreamed a dream of fear
Carved by a jagged spear
In the fabric of my eye, a tear

I dreamed a life like this
Countless sorrows, endless bliss
Carved out of experiences

AT A PARTY

Oh, that lilting mood again
when lyricism slaps like dirty wine
at edges of glasses
and urine wants to flow like words
one should have uttered long ago
(Filthy regrets, dirty wine.)

Drunk and dined,
will-less as a falling star
choiceless as the spinning world
luckless as my own self
derelict as the sky,
I pause for a clear moment
and look out at the night
which is immense.
I cry out from within my skin
at the whole, wide universe:
If you are within me, as they say
reveal yourself, Space!
Darkness of the spinning worlds
twinkling of the stars
turning of the galaxies
in and out of breath

It is I
yes, it is I
who contain you
all the vastness that you are!

MUSIC

Maybe because hearts beat too loud
We have covered ourselves in breaths
Our smells, our sounds

Music has entered into our bodies
A rhythm uncannily found
Loose change lying on the ground

There is music in our being
Spinning us around
We *are* the music
Silence turning into sound

POISON

Desire, Aversion and Delusion: these are the three poisons.

Buddhist teachings

So, if, desire is the poison…
…how convert it into nectar?

I have grappled with desire like a frightened wrestler
beaten from the start, pinned in its throes
with all the failings of a heart;
I have wrestled with it like a body being ravaged
eyes clenched and a fierce
grimace on my face;
I have borne its weight like the chanting of the crows

And all this, what has been,
has been destruction
of an order yet unreachable

Having spoken all that is unhearable
desire withdraws
its claws

POET SHE WHO CAN

To chase these shadows is the lot of my heart
Born to hunt what the rest ignore
Subtle dreams of gore

Hints of meanings or vague disinclinations
Or sudden minute flowerings of the soul
Are all my goal

The lamp from the post
Beams down on the night
I ponder the sight

A poet she who can stand such vision
Darker than darkness itself
Incandescence of human distress

RAIN AND FIRE

All day it has rained the rain of our first desires
The slow, sinuous smoke of still smouldering fires

Desire doesn't die, though hopes get dashed
This fire ever burns, with many tears splashed

Satiation seems close, then again it disappears
A lesson still not learnt, through practice of many years

LISTEN

Listen to me from the site of my silence
Pay good heed to the beat of my heart
Tune into it with art

Listen to the note of nothingness
Striking forever on the drum of the self
A rhythm neither more nor less

Open to the cracks in your being
Spaces of darkness completely freeing
Sights which are beyond all seeing

EVENING

When the sun has turned a lookable red
Through the black branches of a tree
A perfect circular orb and yet
Plunging down to sea

A bird flies across its span
Dark and far-off to the eye
Its wings a flap too tiny and
Inaudible its cry

Turbulence wells up like a boil
In the seething depths of my heart
To cure this sore where find an oil
Where look for lotions to these scars?

DUALITY

Poetry in the midst of all this music
Music in the midst of all this madness
Occasions much sadness

Beauty in the midst of all this ruin
Ruin spread over and surrounded by glory
Makes a sad story

And who are we to be divine or gory
To pursue all this madness or gladness
Gods or devils, beauty/ a bad mess
Vessels of love or a blinded fury?

BLISS

I have tasted great moments of pure being
When I'm not looking, just seeing
Not resisting – agreeing

I have tasted great moments of pure bliss
When a breath is as sweet as a kiss
With nothing to have, and nothing to miss

WHITE EAGLE ON ULLAL BEACH

Your wings in a span of sun-drenched sky
My feet rooted among bones in the sand
Heat off water – vapour, air
My pinched eyes shaded by my hand

The breast is white with coloured wings
But you glide just the same
White eagle is the name I've given you
But wish I could look without a name

WHY?

A steady heartbeat, guaranteed
A bonded labourer, now and then free
What do I want?

A big bank balance, in the vaults
Security with all its bolts
Why do I fret?

A noisy mind, craving for quiet
Extensive rivalry for diet
Why do I live?

SECRET PLACES

Life lives within the cracks in the wall
Those tiny places, those places small
It welters in the wounds of the weak
It groans with those who do not speak

It breathes with the breath of a saint
Life is the plaster peeling off the paint
It sits in silence, and stands in bliss
It flows for the whole duration of a piss

In those cracks within the wall
Light hides its face and lizards crawl
The vast monotony veils those slits
Our secret places, being shred to bits

BREAK

Oh heartbreak, and more heartbreak
to see the beauty of the world
and the frailty of that beauty
and the passing of time
and never stopping to know who one is
and what it all means

At the turn
where the heart breaks
still is the time

RICHLY POOR

Our eyes survey no stars, we're poor
Nothing stirs in the winds of our sighs
No bird spans the horizon of our eyes

Blinded by comfort and murdered by despair
We sing like crows
And fumble like bears

Beggars with limitless delusions of wealth
Feasting in the dumps
On paltry silver crumbs

THE CALL

You called me, so I came
Not hearing precisely what you said
Blind of the beating pulse I made
My way through a crowd of shadows and names

Voices I heard, calls, distresses
Agonies, heartaches of bones in dresses
And when I tried to elbow them away
They nothing could do, had nothing to say

Eyes had faces, thoughts had minds
All dark and dead and covered by blinds
Guided by a lonely phrase I strayed
From where I felt I shouldn't have stayed

With the force of uncomprehended desire
And the urgency a vague memory enjoins
I heard your voice from a far-off point
I entered into the heart of fire

TIME-ZONES

Your night is my afternoon
My evening is your sky
Filled with early morning light

Whether day or dusky twilight
There are endless signals in the sky:
The moon in the afternoon
The glare of the night

ARE YOU THERE?

No, you know that you
Are only half-true
Only half-there
A half shade of blue

You are beyond the pale of reality
Half full of air
Your skin is not flesh because
You can hardly feel a layer

A foot between your legs, and poof!
A blow is dealt to your existence
You only half-exist and that
Only out of sheer persistence

BLISS (2)

Two chairs in a garden and two cups of tea
this is my idea of bliss
two cup-fulls of slurp, and then a kiss…

A KIND OF HAPPENING

I am only a kind of happening
A medium, a trace, a path, a cloud
One of the many who are pushing the crowd
But I am also always unhappening

Things come through me, they're not in my hand
They pass by my finger-tips into the air
I'm a mere channel to prepare
The great white sun that is bursting upon the land

I am, after all, a means to no end
A via-media for all the nothings of the world
That hurtle along, or else madly are hurled
I am the story—no beginning—no end

Note: Inspired from the phrase, "A way of happening," in W. H.
Auden's *In Memory of W.B. Yeats*.

CLOTHESLINE

Wet clothes on a clothesline
dripping water, dripping sweat
hanging out in the sun to dry
from hands putting them out to rest

Arms extend, contract, extend
as new clothes join the old on the line
hands clip them up, and spread them out
it is so peaceful in the morning at nine

All these women, they're all my sisters
they're all my mothers, all my lovers
these women who every morning try
to place the clothes neatly on the line to dry

The rope round my neck is also a line
as I sit in the sun and sputter and die
I choke on my emotions while breakfast readies
I stretch out my feet, to look and sigh

Winter mornings I sit in my balcony
a balcony that is five floors high
and observe all the clotheslines around me
lines dripping with wet clothes to dry

lines dripping with wet clothes to dry

lines dripping ... wet clothes, dry...
lines...

WORDS HAVE BECOME TREES

We do not speak much now
we only make love
words are left far behind and we
are travelling on a road where we have rested
from time to time

Silence is already here, in this night
the chirping of the crickets allows
my hand to touch her cheek and lie
inertly like a shroud

Our wandering's end is a promised land
there is nothing there
only, words have become trees
and the grass
an infinite silence

TIMES OF DEATH

In times of death silence reigns

I think of pain and I think of rain
As rhymes to go with 'reigns'
Or maybe chains

But death is too vast a valley
For me to speak of chains
Maybe pain…
Maybe walking in the rain
Head down and heart heavy
And eyes full of pain

Death has come to this valley and rained
In red
All the right rhymes are stained

I LONG TO WEAVE

I long to weave
the fabric of your skin
into my dreams and fly
on the carpet of your hair

There must be a reply
somewhere
in your heart to all this

I long to sleep
on the bed of your kiss

A PRAYER FOR LOVERS

Lord give them peace
The world is not what they want it to be
Laughter and bliss and ease
How could it be?

O Master, please
Their hearts are brittle like their knees
Any cruelty runs them down
A silence threatened by any sound

O Spirit, let them be
So tightly bound and yet so frail
A soothing stillness setting sail
On blindly violent seas

O Giver of life, O Figure of love
Move our paths to love, oh move
That we may be silent as they are
And laugh together in your power
Free of all our worldly scars
From hour to hour
And hour to hour

WILL YOU CALL IT HELL?

Will you call it hell, this everyday life
Soothing and banal as a kitchen-knife
Some call it fate and some our age
All I could call it is not on my page

In a blindfold alley where everything is seen
I shut my mouth to open my skin
Porous at surface and empty within
A traveller of hell in all its inns

And yet untouched, just like a fire
I go through motion with a clearer mind
A silent courser in hell's entire
Heaven that's left behind

SILENCE

Silence is praise
Lord, my soul is as deep as a river
As dense as a maze

I lie in wait like a wanted criminal
Watch in the dark
The leaves are still and there is silence in the park

My eyes glow like lamps without shades
A cat is beside me
In the silence of these glades

O these stars, all shards of my heart
Which yearns to take you in like the night
Now the sound of the silence is right

Hear! – Did you hear? – I heard its sigh
It moans like a beast
And drones like a fly

Silence is close by
Creeping and rolling like waves of the night
For once my thieving heart hears right

LETTER

I resign hereby from the offices of thought
It were too much for me to continue as I ought
Thinking and planning and calculating a lot
So here I resign from the offices of thought

Deep into a different world I'll venture
Trust in that capital, shares and debenture
Deep into a different world I'll go
Where debts are long and recovery slow

I formally accept the post of a recluse
I promise to put all my powers to use
To roam in the myriad mirrors of the muse
Where images are bright and reflection obtuse

UNTITLED

Dark blood lights up the sky
like fireworks
in the middle of the night there is a landscape burning
as the contours of a heart melt and dry
in the cold desert aridity
a far-off lie
gives vent to near feelings
a mad mood sparks off in the sky
and off they fly
the lids of the heavens
Brooding

DELIGHT

When you first brought the day into light
conjured it with a prayer
juggled it in your hands
and whipped it up like cream:

And when you said, 'What a wonderful sight!'
and served me up your impeccable smile
as you waited for me to taste:

I wondered for a silly while
looking at this day wrenched from night,
I wondered what it would be like
to lick the corners of this light:

And then you put your tongue to mine,
loud I cried—delight! delight!

UNTIL

Far have I wandered the corners of this earth
A travelling madman with hair overgrown
With eyes overblown from sights of wonder
And feet overtorn

Long have I waited at this corner of my heart
Long have I tended the wings of this desire
Stationary and still, quiet until
I catch fire

UNDOING

Grab a piece of the sky, dilute
Its thickness with your tears, then try
To mix it well with air, because
You don't know what you're doing why

It's normal, fit and understandable
To not know what you're doing why
So mix it well with air, because
Let's have some bubbles before you're dry

Take a piece of your heart and pound
It thoroughly with your head that's shaken
Lick a little of the resulting compound
To learn at last that you were mistaken

FACADES

Every lipstick is an advertisement
And every eye a lie
A twinkle of diamonds and demands in the sky

Every cloth is a rag
And all nudity a blind
To pin us behind the veil of the mind

Every hand wears a grip
And is a threat to our throat
A smoulder of desire in the night and the note

Every dollar has a din
And a damn behind it
We swear by our money sir, please don't mind it

Every laugh is a joke
And all anguish a riot
If it's on a card, then we can buy it

All speech is a knife
Deeper into ourselves
Let's make merry cheer and jangle some bells

All happiness is a rouge
On the sickness of our cheeks
Reality blinks through botches and leaks

DESIRE IS ALREADY MEMORY

Pray crush this ice so it bleed no more
I've wept enough for lost desires
Flatten it out and lay it to the floor

The poking of the croaking fires
Retrieves a live ember from the stones
But all my embers are liars

The glow calmly smoking from the bones
Aches like a book in inadequate light
Fruits of expectation are born

Memories charge like riders in the night
And reach toward a distant shore
For selves that are forever out of sight

Note: The title is a line from Italo Calvino's *Invisible Cities*.

SELF-OBSERVATION

Turning a careful eye
On the blind spots of the self
I see dust on the shelf

In the pits of these shadows
Lies the dirt
We wish to escape unhurt

The miasma of these marshes
Chokes up the throat
I drown in shallow moats

Honesty is hard
Nakedness is scary
We prefer to stay airy

Who can really see themselves?
Who can really bear to look?
Who can suffer to read this book?

The night is long
And we are soon too old
To dig for gold

THE BEGGAR'S SONG

Lend your hand in love or a slap
Our destinies are one
A stitch in the gap
Made or undone

Big Hard Policeman
Swinging your baton
And you on your cellphone
Who won't even look at me

Business and Crime lord the earth
Where rage and despair have hungered long
Mere metal for my song, dear Sir?
How about a look, a touch?

JOURNEY TO EDEN

When the throes of evil subside
And if
Let us head for places that abide
In bliss

Hands that hurt with malignant skill
And women who nag too frustrated to shout
Are the things that lie without
Are the bite of the bitter pill

Sheltering in the shade of our tree
Sinking into the depths of our ocean
Let us taste the fruits of true devotion
Let us sing in order to see

A man may in this knowledge kneel
Fulfilled, this true emotion feel
We're bound only to be free

SPACETIME

Space was just an abstraction around me
Until I felt its hands
On my throat, choking me down
I tried my best to counter with a frown
Space spread its arms and beautifully bound me
I guess you could say it found me
It raised me up and flattened me like the sands

I made love to space as I would to a woman
I went all tense inside it
And found release and ease
Oh peace!
I felt I would always make
Love to a woman
As I would to space

I have always been in love with space
But not so much with time
As my life has gathered pace
It has lost its rhythm, or rhyme
There is not space enough for embrace
There is no gesture adequate for a sign

I crave more space and nothing of time
Bounding on in a blinding race
Running bleakly
Through ragged ways

At the bottom of the ocean I know a place
Far, far away from sunshine's rays

A little to the left, within the slime
Where days dig deeper as if they were grace
And moments unfold, as if all of time

THE GARDEN

Walk into the garden of my attention
I welcome you with an open smile
Release your self and ease all my tension
Come into my garden and walk a while

Waltz into the arenas of intention
Dance with your gaze, sway with your smile
Swing to my breath and release all tension
Open the locks on your heart awhile

Let us leave these arid deserts of inattention
Tend to the garden, water it fertile
Release our selves and gain infinite attention
Bloom, take root, branch out, reconcile

UNDER A TREE, BY THE SEA, IN PONDICHERRY

I saw the sunlight splinter
on the back of my hand
at the edge of the sea
and through my fingers
I saw it on the bark of a tree

It split and glittered
and glittered and split
The water shimmered
so brightly mirrored
so whitely slivered
that in fact I spluttered
and fell out of my seat

Maybe there was too much heat.
My hand on my mouth
I swallowed it out
maybe I had too much to eat.

The sunlight shivered
and continued to repeat.

FEEL

Do you know what I fear?

At the brittle surface of my skin
All the bottled-up stuff within
Is beginning to appear

Can you guess at what I dread?

By the watery edge of my eyes
One foot in and the other out
I smoke in my sighs
Drag out my doubts
Recall the things I never said

Do you know how I feel?

I don't think I know how I feel
The surface of my skin, which is beginning to peel
Curls and dries up in the heat
At once I apprehend my startling feat
I don't really know how I feel

Is this all there is?

Not knowing what there is
I wonder at the unplumbed depths
Lying unrevealed

A storm of emotions
May rage on the surface
But the mystery keeps singing softly
Secretly in my ear, Friend
You don't know what it is to feel

A PRAYER

What is it that I search like this
With such unbearably haunted eyes
What is it that I miss?

So much breeds within me I don't know
From what strange soil these creatures grow
Grasping and seething
Disconsolate
Avaricious

The sky is soft and sudden today
Clear blue, yet evening cloudy
And my heart is like a slate wiped clean
Of the figures of imagination

O demons of the heart
I know you have to claim your part
Your portion of our flesh
Our blood, our mind, our all too human
Mess

So scare me but spare me
In my fragile humanness
Confiscate with art
All that I must confess
But leave me just the tiny part
To drink my share of the silent sky
In grateful peace and emptiness

ALL THAT YOU COULD NOT SAY

I despair of my silences.
Twilight mourning death of the sun.

Termite of my memories
bites me hollow from within
I stare at the sun
through the glass of my skin
ponder the course I've run
and the person I've been

Shouldn't I have been more brittle
to break down into words, sentences
like silly little mechanical toys
twisted, deformed by discontented boys?

My eyes would weep for shame,
but they fail.
Silent hordes roll over these ways
relentless unrelenting waves
of mechanical self-pity;
this is where all ends meet
this is where the past repeats
this is where humanity converges
this is where our sanity verges
on the borders of unsanitised dream:
the City

My cheek swells like an unforgiven page.
All that could not be spoken
all the still unbroken
pieces of a shattered glass
cannot conjure a revealing phrase

A poet is silenced by his words.
We are made wounded
by all that we could not say.

Even as we speak we fail
to say it
We fail to articulate our condition
and are as if we never existed.

NIGHT FELL LIKE RAIN

Night fell like rain
Encumbered like a thought
And it weighed, like emotion
And it stayed, unsought
In-wrought
Like you

Night fell like rain, pattered
Seeped into my mind, it mattered
Steadily, like you

Night fell like rain
Heart dripped like dew
All that time, oh all that time
I soaked in you

THAT

The one enduring thought of my life
The point at its centre, the hole at its goal
My only bliss, my sole tormentor
You take your toll

To think of you is to recall
Extreme emotion like pounding rain
Spreading wide its open arms
Like a cracked windowpane

My mind is like a bloated body
Floating on a swollen river
There is a flood in the tides of men
Every summer or every winter

Can one really say what *that* is?
It is what it's meant to be
The point at its goal, the hole in the centre
Stranded ship on a boundless sea

MODERN LOVE

Come smear this anguish-laden heart of mine
With the blood of your lipstick, our love:
Paint it in a corner vividly
Or splash it around like a bottle of wine

Encapsulate its scars and scoop up its sighs
Into big dollops of dolorous dyes

Put it on a billboard, gouge out my eyes
Enlegend our love, my love—advertise

MARKETPLACE

We won't let love just be
We won't let *anything* just be
We take our turn-ons so seriously

Newspaper emotions and agony spreadsheets
Measure heartbeats
Analyse our teats

Discourse lengthens out like a wave
Voices crave
For soundless caves

Reality and dream mingle and bend
In a solid blend
Of buy and vend

I WATCH IT EVERY DAY

I watch it every day,
      they're cutting trees
Hacking them to death,
      it is painful to behold
(Some are stolen,
      some are sold to the road)

Its legs beheaded
      and crippled for life
A bald stump frowns,
      squints up at the sky
(Cars are visible,
      but I have no eyes)

Death everyday is painful to behold
Murder stays young, while I grow old.

IN THE MODERN MADHOUSE

In the modern madhouse I saw
Painted houses with deleterious streets
Policemen on their beats

Words proliferate like opinions on love
With nothing to state
Words frustrate

Stars still spill from the skies above
Our begging bowls elsewhere are bared
Unprepared

In the modern madhouse my jaw
Came unstuck and dropped to the ground
Happiness I found?

NOBODY

In the land of Nobody I dwell
Where I live Nobody dresses too well
Nobody is always shouting out loud
Nobody makes No-one very proud
Nobody studies, Nobody fails
Nobody kills and goes to jail
Nobody builds forts, drives a car
To work or sleep, Nobody goes far
Nobody cares for image, keeps in style
Nobody has a fixed smile
Nobody slogs or hogs or fights
Nobody passes lonely nights
Nobody's angry, Nobody's sad
Nobody calls Nobody mad
Nobody's a woman, Nobody's a man
Nobody subscribes to a chauvinist clan
I hate Nobody, Nobody hates me
In the land of Nobody I'm free.

SHADOW PLAY

Life is short, your memory long
In the lengthening shadow I see
Your eyes smiling back at me

The curve of your lips is like a song
That I am slowly learning to sing
A new bird that is taking wing

In my arms you do nothing wrong
Your breath inspires in me the strength
To lay out in all our shadow's length

EMPTINESS

In the obtuse angles of my thought
Fell a shaft of light
All gleamy and dreamy but straight
Insight

In the tentacled corners of my being
Moved a little claw
First stirrings of a yet unrealised
Flaw

I could see where my arms were headed
In the strangest spaces of the void
In a cushy fullness embedded
And devoid

A RAVEN CAME TO WISH ME LUCK

A raven came to wish me luck
Ugly and shining black
It gave me everything I wanted
Without the option of giving it back

It flapped its wings, I slipped and stuttered
Its eyes were grim and sharply black
It saw me turn the way I wanted
Without the option of turning back

It alighted on my heavy heart
And built a nest like a blighted blanket
Black holes like coins stuffed each part
I had no voice to really thank it

DO NOT GO GENTLE

"Do not go gentle into that good night."
I wish I could go gentle into the night
After each petty day
Whirring like a jammed engine
Shredding the nerves

The turning of the page each day
To find a missing alphabet there
Printers' devils find voice in disappearance
Hunt for the black pen here
To fill in the void thereabouts
Or find a whole page blank or two.

The tensions of wriggling through each day
Like a worm in the brain, decaying the brain
Eroding the heart

Let me have only so much each day
That I may go gentle into each night.

And not like the shrivelling day...but

Unengined

Note: The title and first line refer to Dylan Thomas's famous poem,
"Do Not Go Gentle Into That Good Night."

SHUDDER & EXIST

In life my love took
An awkward turn
Into nothingness

*

Was it worth it
To have looked after me such a long time
Precariously?

*

Waiting for the night to be right
Before the sight
Of a million booming stars set free

*

To be or not to be
The twisters have always been there
Unaware

*

"Roles, roles, some brand new roles for you, Sir!
Fresh, piping hot, safely within quotes;
For in old roles don't we grow old?"

*

All the world's a stage and we
Unfortunately
Are not in the audience

*

Depth in high seas largely unlooked for
Feels neglected
And wonders if it's there

*

All ships are born to totter at sea
Like fish
That are learning to swim

*

Stars should be kept under one's will
Held with an iron hand—
Or they forget to wriggle and twinkle

*

"Tell me, tell me, have you seen my frog
Has bulging eyes, and slime on his body?"–
"Ma'am, that fugitive has escaped our bog."

*

Poetry is a useless thing
Except for those who read it
And those compelled to write

*

Blood drying through all my body
Blood draining out of my mind
Blanched relief, the residue

*

Love and death are almost synonyms
Being and meaning almost there but not quite
And escape is a mere word that I write

*

O moon how inconstant art thou
Now sublime now prostitute
Like me

*

Every spasm lets out three lines
That shudder & exist, and encompass a world
Wrapped in nothingness

*

Sex flows from me to you,
From you to me:
That is how it's incomplete —

MUSIC (2)

Music that in these words flows
Is a wave to be caught in
To be brought in
To you

Presented
On a platter
To be patted.

EXIT!

Exit, pursued by a bear.[1] What a way to go!
One might have (reasonably) expected
An ounce of relief, to be off-stage
One might even have understood despair
The final despair of not knowing what one has been

But this! 'Exit, pursued by a bear!'
Most ridiculous, ungainly, undignified
What a way to have to pretend to die
What a way to bid good-bye
To exit the stage, running, pursued by a bear!

The very lights would have been amazed
At not being given a chance to fade
And the bear would have wondered
What is this ridiculous thing that I chase
And why should *I* be put on-stage?

---

[1] From the play *The Winter's Tale* by William Shakespeare.

TWILIGHT

The chill is not great. I am warm.
Light is fading with the fading sun.

The earth's serenely in its course
The calm descends with mighty force.

Birds have settled. Buildings are calm.
Cars are home (those that can).

All is still. So very silent.
The air empty, yet carries the scent

Of memories. Harmony
Dances tonight on its toes for me.

Peace that passeth understanding.
A mystic joy informs the evening.

My skull still sucks the air in
And greets the world with its hideous grin.

LOVE SONG FOR A LONELY NIGHT

Light fell like petals in dreams
Or visions of the late afternoon.
Come back soon, my love, come back soon!

I began to work the book of my hours
Waiting by some waiting shore.
Haven't we met before?

Evening entered the city like a dog
Looking for a place to sit and expire.
Come on baby, light my fire!

Rivers, breaths and hours run
Tumbling into the night of the sea.
O my love, where could you be?

The clock on the wall, the beats of my watch
Time my run into tomorrow.
O, baby – you're the cause of my sorrow!

A MOOD PIECE

Crows descending on scarlet flowers.
Aye, the spell is upon me again
I'll sing and write my darkest hours.

The cawing fills the reddening air
Colours threaten to flood in from the sides
I move to touch the black of my hair.

Sootiness is the flavour of the age.
O ye who know not how ye live
Why don't you cry, why don't you rage?

Blood and thunder fill the sky —
But wait, and let me not dramatize
My rotten putrid apples of the eye.

'Beauty', 'Love' and 'Sadness' make
My sweet red heart crack and crumble
Like icing on a chocolate cake.

Crows' feet radiate from the reds of my eyes
Peering still for a way to survive
Our massive machine of automatic sighs

LOVER

I crave his body like nothing else in the world.

Tenderness is what I feel for him
Tenderness runs through my body
blood, water, arteries, veins
Tenderness is the hair on my body –
for him they surge.
He is my whim and my every urge,
the dark silence that I carry
like a wallet folded within my heart,
or a memory curled.

I crave his body like nothing else in the world.
I brave my own fate
And I make love of all this hate.

VAN GOGH

I

The pattern of all artistic endeavour.
A sight for the ages to ponder.

Self-disgust in the broken ear
Dispassionate eyes and regard
(Heart thumping and grinding away—
ignored).
A brush with life, canvas
for a million stars, their zooming
orbits and ellipses that gleam
deep into the dark night of the soul.
Romanticism
refusing to die or be reviled:
Flowers!
Yellow, brown, beautiful brilliant flowers!
Brightness of the dark painful hours
an intense sense of loneliness
devolving into black liquid night:
Madness.
The quiet room with wooden planks for floor
A stray chair (like a dog)
Don't breathe the air here
or gather the nuts of a wilting personality...

Fade, fade, self-efface
A gun that makes a lot of noise
A madhouse without its central poise
Paint and drink to its last bitter dregs
This life, drain off and die.

II

Was a preacher once, never knew
how to paint or stuff
like that. Thought life was meant to be lived
to some good and generations
hereafter to come.
Searched with haunted eyes
hidden corners of the light
for things that didn't exist. (Looking for a — just one —meaning
of life. Didn't find.)
So I painted. So I tried.
Dark and bony sighs.
Poverty and its cries.

But that is that and past is past
before I went to the South of France
and discovered life. Shady
aspects of light.
Hunted all we collectively hide
drew contrasts, and lived a life
beyond regret or recall.
     I died.

III

These sweet sonatas
Are the beauty of Art.
They touch the heart.

These silent strokes
Express distress
In colourful dress.

My life is lived
My passions spent—
My art intent.

RELATIONSHIP

You have ways
In which you want my eyes to see
In which you'd rather have me be

I have ways
My whole life has gone into making
Which there is no forsaking

CRITICALITY

In the middle of an unspeakable sentence
I pause to analyse it
and dissect and trash it
and slash it to bits and pieces and cut it
and pierce it to lace it with all the agony of my being
and lash it

But I can't make words
bear the burden of my darkness
and yet that is all I incessantly seek to do.

MUST HAVE BEEN

I must have been born a woman in past life
For I can completely grasp how it feels
And tear these feelings off peel by peel
I who was my husband's devoted wife
I must have been born a woman in past life

I must have committed a lot of good deeds
Like running an endless circle in my head
And soldiering on when I might have been dead
A thousand roses spawn while the life-spirit bleeds
I must have committed a lot of good deeds

I must have known how to inhabit this body
To smile in spite of all at the play of my child
I might have been submissive, or maybe even wild
In response to your violence, but hardly ever shoddy
I must have known how to inhabit this body

I must have been all you wanted me to be
Silly or sweet, a carnal black hole
I must have essayed every possible role
I must have looked hard when you told me to see
I must have been all you wanted me to be

I must have done well to now be a man
To have so much power, to have so much pride
All this to defend, and you for a bride
I have found freedom, but not as I planned
Just a different place in hell, to now be a man

Poems
Solitary Beyond Time
[2010-2012]

Selection of poems published in 2012 by Akademie Schloss Solitude in Stuttgart, Germany, as *Allein Jenseits Der Zeit* with German translations.

THE TRAVELLER

Here I am
a traveller in nowhere and no place
doing nothing

at no time, with no body
asking nothing

not the way to a place
nor the hour of the day

seeking nothing
no shrine, no temple, no mountain, no lake

I am
doing nothing
a traveller on his way…

I AM...

a dreamer caught in reality
eternity caught in time
a desert caught in an oasis
a poem caught in a rhyme

I am that which cannot be
What I am cannot be told
I am that and this is me
This was I but that is old.

POETRY

Poetry is work of the soul
Product of many hours of emptiness
Rare as a caress

I have no words to describe it
How it happens, how it's done
The root comes to fruit when the tree's broken

People ask me, "What do you do?" but
I have no words to describe it
'Nothing' almost fits the description
Then a poem comes to spoil the fun.

POETRY (2)

This, then, is true art:
to not know what I'm saying
and yet be able to say it

I say it and I don't say it.
You know and you don't know.

This, then, is really art:
that which happens unknowing, unsaying
from me to you.

THE VIRGIN

In the light of that summer I saw the leaking winter
come down to its knees, beg and plead
and melt away without hope of shelter
from the gaze of a sun that was sprouting a seed

So, as I age, my youth looks upon me
killing hopes of wisdom, experiences, that greed
that held me frozen, a virgin in a swelter
to lose her name, but unwilling to bleed.

ACKNOWLEDGEMENTS

With deep gratitude to:

Sushma, Smriti and Shabnam, the deadly trio that brought *Bleed* to life! My mom and sis, for their unflagging love and support. Sheetal, Namrata, Sandeep, Sushma, Meera, Bela, Smriti, Rangeeta, Shikha, Khushboo, Lina, Shruti, Prem, Nina, Dhruv dada and Shabnam, for forming a select band of avid readers with whom these poems were first shared via a small email group. Nomita, Shreya, Juhi and Neha, for the love and affirmation.

Jane Sahi, for agreeing to write a generous and warm foreword to the collection.

Ravi Ravindra, for reading and also writing a brief review.

Akademie Schloss Solitude, Stuttgart, Germany, for my time there in 2010-11 and for publishing a first collection of poems, some of which are shared here.

Hawakal Publishers for their belief in the book, and loving attention to detail.

ABOUT THE AUTHOR

Vipul is an un-pin-downable free spirit — a traveller, poet, novelist, singer, dancer, meditator, and seeker. He has cultivated over the years a deep taste for the ordinary, an ability to savour the simple in each moment. A man's true wealth is his "time," Vipul says, and he stays resolutely "rich" in this regard. He has been fellow for literature at the Akademie Schloss Solitude in Germany in 2010-11, and he has published a novel (*2012 Nights*), a book of poems (*Solitary Beyond Time*), and short stories. Since 2012 Vipul has plunged into the world of *bhakti* poetry and music with the Kabir Project, journeying into the oral traditions in villages, doing translations and original writing for two forthcoming books and a web archive. A *tambura* came along as a gift, and he has taken to the joy of singing himself, interpreting and sharing these songs with diverse audiences. His love for *bhakti* music notwithstanding, Vipul Rikhi has a hidden and formidable knowledge of old Hindi film songs. And, be it tango or *garba*, he loves to dance.